More Crazy — But True!

JONATHAN CLEMENTS has been a collector of curious and fantastic facts ever since he discovered that it is illegal to eat snakes in Iran on Sundays. *More Crazy-But True!* is a sequel to *Crazy-But True!*, published in Armada, and the author has also compiled *The Armada Book of Jokes and Riddles*, *The Great British Quiz Book*, and *Lucky for You!*, a zany guide to fortune-telling. Jonathan Clements is a full-time writer and photographer, and lives with his wife in Wiltshire.

ROGER SMITH produces television commercials for a large advertising agency. His artistic talents were first spotted while he was doodling on his office wallpaper. He is an illustrator in his spare time, and lives in London with his wife and two children.

Jonathan Clements

with drawings by Roger Smith

AN ORIGINAL ARMADA

Also in Armada by Jonathan Clements:

Crazy-But True!
The Armada Book of Jokes and Riddles
The Great British Quiz Book
Lucky for You!

in the same series:

1st, 2nd & 3rd Armada Books of Fun
1st & 2nd Armada Books of Cartoons
Fun On Wheels

More Crazy-But True!
was first published in Armada in 1976
by William Collins Sons & Co. Ltd.
14 St James's Place, London SW1A 1PF

Printed in Great Britain by
William Collins Sons & Co. Ltd.
London & Glasgow

Contents

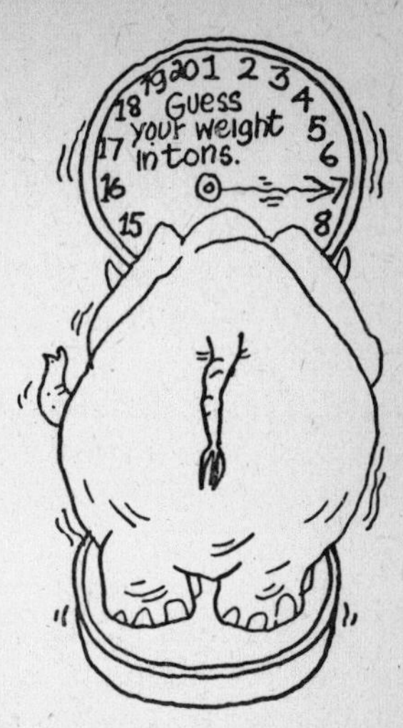

'What Has Four Knees, an Ivory Moustache and Weighs Seven Tons?'

Ahah – caught you! For the title of this first chapter isn't a riddle, but a straightforward question. And the answer is – an elephant. What's more, the elephant is the only animal in the world with four knees. Which goes to prove that you can learn something new every day, even if it might seem useless and crazy. (In fact, a lot of things you'll learn from this book *are* useless and crazy, but we won't go into that now.)

Astonishing news to make you tremble with excitement . . . this book is chock-full of hundreds of strange and crazy facts like the case of the four-kneed elephant. For example, did you know that the orang-outang has lines on the palms of its hand exactly like a human being?

You can do whatever you like with this storehouse of valuable information – win friends and influence bishops, astound and shock passers-by in the street, win prizes in odd quiz games, torture your parents, and even grow hair on bald elbows (see chapter '*How to Grow Hair on Bald Elbows*'). In time, you'll wonder how you ever managed to survive without a copy of *More Crazy-But True!* ... or how you are *going* to survive now you have got one.

But now it's time to enjoy yourself. Dive into the following fund of crazy and stupefying facts, and don't forget to dry your eyes when you come out ...

The figure 4 is the only number having as many letters as its meaning: four.

Snowflakes measuring 17 inches across fell in Montana, U.S.A., in February 1887.

The Ancient Greeks invented the yo-yo.

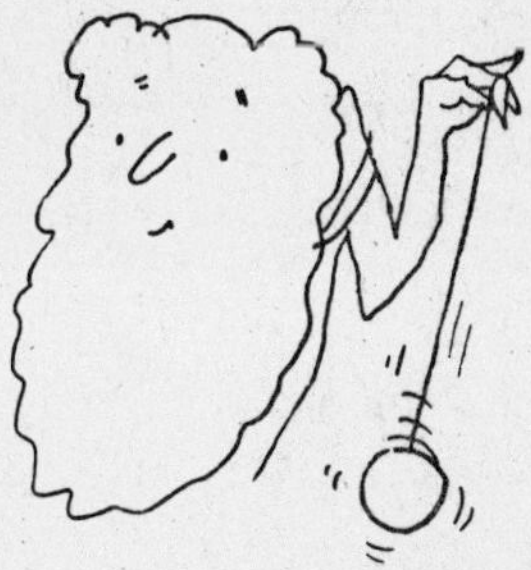

Queen Elizabeth I created an office called 'The Official Uncorker Of Sea-Bottles', after a fisherman in Cornwall found an important official secret in a bottle washed up on the beach. Any person not handing over such bottles to the Officer was liable to be hanged.

The rhinoceros's horn isn't horn at all. It's made of hair so compact that it's as hard as bone.

Duelling is legal in Uruguay – providing both parties are registered blood-donors.

To illustrate a lecture on marine biology at St John's College, Minnesota, U.S.A., Professor Daniel Kaiser swallowed 257 live minnows.

In the 18th century, a kipper was a dried and cured salmon. In the 19th century, it was a cod. Nowadays, it's a dried and cured herring.

Cold water is heavier than hot water.

'Machoumaerobilengmonoolemongametsoarobilengmono-olemong' means '99' in the language of the Basutos tribe of Africa.

In 1968, Daventry Council paid their official rat-catcher £7.75 compensation after he had lost his spectacles down a large rat hole.

There are 12,000,000 cells in the human brain.

The French language has a vocabulary of nearly 100,000 words – less than half the English vocabulary.

General Trevor Townsend, of London, could control the palpitation of his heart, and suspend its action whenever he wanted to. He proved this in a public demonstration, attended by two notable doctors – Dr Cheyne and Dr Bayard, in 1857. General Townsend died eight days after suspending his heart action in 1861.

One cubic mile of sea-water contains approximately seven million tons of Epsom salts.

Edward VII used to weigh his guests after weekends at Sandringham, to make sure they had eaten well and gained weight.

Of Great Britain's 97,000 postmen, approximately 3,000 were bitten by dogs in 1974.

The very first Girl Guide was Allison Cargill, a Glasgow schoolgirl. When she was denied membership of the Boy Scouts in 1908, she started her own group called the 'Cuckoo Patrol'.

You cannot buy Virginia cigarettes in Virginia, U.S.A. All the tobacco grown there is used for export.

In 16th century England, bachelors were required by law to be indoors by 9 pm.

Rudyard Kipling's famous poem 'If' first appeared in *The Times* Obituary Column in 1917, as a tribute to his friend, Dr Jameson.

Snow isn't white – it's transparent. It is composed of tiny crystals, each with six sides. The rays of light. reflected by the various surfaces, give snow its impression of glistening whiteness.

The sponge isn't a plant. It's an animal.

The fastest-moving snail in Great Britain is 'Lightning', who lives in Falmouth, Cornwall. Lightning's record journey is two feet, travelled in 80 seconds.

Circus tights were invented by an American bare-back rider, Nelson Hower, in 1828, when he appeared in his underwear after his costume failed to arrive. The fashion caught on.

Cleopatra wasn't Egyptian. She was a Greek, the daughter of Ptolemy Auletes.

In Germany there is a species of flea, the dottheimer, which only lives and breeds inside beer-mats in pubs.

If letter-writers address their envelopes in very scrawly, babylike handwriting, affix a Toyland Post Office Stamp, and post it in Her Majesty's Mails, the Postmaster General is obligated to see that the letter is delivered.

The engineers of the M5 Motorway to Exeter have built the smallest underpass in the world – a tunnel one foot wide to allow badgers to get safely to the other side.

Only the female mosquito bites: the male of the species is not equipped for biting.

A certain Mr Roberts, of Evesham, claimed a record in 1971 after walking for 32 minutes with four live ferrets inside his trousers.

30,000 people – mainly innocent old women – were burned at the stake in Europe during the years 1621-1640, for supposedly practising witchcraft.

The Emperor of Rome from 161-192, Commodus Lucius Aurelius, was also a prize-fighter and won 1,131 fights in the Gladiator's Arena. He was finally strangled to death by a wrestler.

In the 18th century, butchers were called 'Flesh-Floggers'.

The Earl of Stirling, Sir William Alexander (1567-1640), received from King James I the country of Canada. The yearly rent for the entire country was one penny – payable on Christmas Day.

The Australian bush-turkey collects about five tons of leaves and twigs to build its huge nest.

The Apples and Oranges of the Species

Strangers often stop me in the street and ask me just where I get all this crazy information from. (Often they stop me in the street and hit me over the head with a brick, but that's another story.) But whenever people do stop me, I always – after putting on a crash-helmet to be safe – give them the same answer.

Crazy information comes from everywhere. From drains and dustbins, from backstreets in exotic Japan, from the lips of literary roadsweepers in Soho, even from the backs of buses. I scour the surface of the globe for weird facts. Sometimes I am to be found wandering in the Gobi desert; sometimes I am to be found up a tree in Sherwood Forest, counting all sorts of odd things. Sometimes I can't be found at all – then I presume I'm lost, and I sit down and sulk. (This is usually the case.) But somehow I always manage to return from my expeditions with some weird and wonderful news to startle the world and make people gasp with wonder. Quite often they gasp with wonder – or horror – that I manage to return at all.

So now you know the background secrets, and the ceaseless toil that goes into the making of a great big lump of crazy facts, like the following . . .

Chinese and Japanese babies are born with a blue mark on their bottoms, which disappears after about two years.

The tailor bird of India gets its name from its singular method of nesting. It selects a large leaf, and carefully sews the sides together, using fibre as thread, and in the pocket it creates, builds its nest.

Lady Macbeth had a son called Lulach the Fatuous.

The Daimler 'Conquest' car owed its name to its original price, before purchase tax, of £1,066.

A man was treated in a Kuala Lumpur hospital for a badly sprained neck after a trained monkey, sent up a tree to gather coconuts, jumped on to his shoulders and began unscrewing his head.

John Trundley, known as the 'Great Fat Lad of Peckham Rye', was born in 1899. At the age of eleven he weighed 28 stone.

Dan Fletcher, an American, has invented a motorised pogo-stick. It runs on two-stroke fuel, and gives about 30,000 hops – nearly fifty miles – to the gallon.

The famous artist Picasso's full name was: Pablo Diego Jose Francisco de Paula Juan Nepomuceno Maria de los Remedios Cipriano de la Santissima Trinidad Ruiz Picasso.

In 1967, a Prague housewife, Vera Czemsk, jumped out of her sixth-storey bedroom window when she learned that her husband was planning to run away from her. She recovered in hospital after landing on top of her husband – who was killed outright.

Buildings over 100 feet high lean slightly towards the course of the sun.

Garden midges beat their wings approximately 1,000 times a second.

It can be so cold in Verkhoyansk, Siberia, that boiling water poured from a kettle would be turned to solid ice as soon as it reached the ground.

The first Poet Laureate of England was a Frenchman, Henri d'Avranches, who lived during the rein of Henry I.

Sir Winston Churchill's last words were: 'Oh, I am so *bored* with it all.'

An official Government handbook, published in 1968, announced that one of the most efficient ways of scaring birds away from airports was to: 'Stand silhouetted on the skyline and, by raising and lowering the extended arms laterally in a rhythmic fashion about twenty-four times a minute, thus imitating the wing-beat action of an eagle'.

Rabbits have been known to reach a speed of 47 m.p.h.

A member of the Holmshill Old Boys' football team hit an opponent in the face during a match in 1971. He was not only booked by the referee, but also successfully prosecuted. The opposing team were the St Alban's City Police – who lost the match 1–4.

One in every five of Birmingham's policemen is married to a nurse.

Table-tennis, when it was first invented by James Gibb in 1926, was first called 'Gossamer'.

The word 'typewriter' uses only the letters on a typewriter's top row of letter keys.

The brain of modern man is approximately $1\frac{1}{2}$ inches smaller than that of Neanderthal Man.

20-year-old Sandy Allen, the world's tallest woman at 7 feet 5 inches, had her first date when a 7 foot 2 inch man drove all the way from Illinois to Indiana to take her out. For dinner, Sandy had ten shrimp cocktails, six large steaks, a triple banana split and eight double portions of ice-cream cake.

The world's biggest bell is in the Kremlin in Moscow. It weighs 198 tons, but has never been rung – it was severely cracked whilst being cast.

Panama hats aren't made in Panama. They are made from the large leaf of the Cardulavia plant of South America, and are manufactured mainly in Buenos Aires and Manchester.

There are approximately five hundred million spiders in Great Britain.

The word 'curate' should really be applied to a vicar, and vice-versa. For 'curate' is derived from the Latin '*curatus*', meaning one having charge of souls; and 'vicar' from the Latin '*vicarius*', meaning deputy or substitute.

Sir Walter Raleigh's widow carried her husband's embalmed head wherever she travelled until she died, nearly 29 years after Sir Walter's execution.

In the eight years between 1601 and 1609, two thousand French noblemen died whilst fighting duels.

King Charles I was only 4 feet 7 inches tall.

The energy released by the heat of a cow's belches in just one day would be sufficient to generate central heating in an average-sized house for over a week.

It is a criminal offence in Britain, punishable by a term of five years' imprisonment, to 'riotously demolish a hovel'.

Birmingham has 22 more miles of canal than Venice.

The most popular active sport played by adults in Great Britain is darts.

It is impossible for the Queen to be late for the ceremony of Trooping the Colour. There is an officer with the special task of putting back the clock if ever she should be.

One of the display stands at the Institute of Personnel Management Conference in the Exhibition Hall, Harrowgate, in 1974, was that of the Royal Society for the Prevention of Accidents. The stand collapsed.

A female bed-bug once survived for 620 days without food.

When Rowland Hill first had the idea of a 'piece of paper just large enough to bear the Crown's stamp, and covered at the back with a kind of glue, with which the bringer might, by applying a little moisture, attach it to the front of a letter', he met with a great deal of opposition. The then Postmaster General, Lord Lichfield, publicly expressed his disapproval of the idea thus: 'Why, of all the wild, crackpot and idiotic schemes I have ever heard of, this is the most foolish and extravagant! The man Hill should be horse-whipped!'

Diovanni Rossi, an Italian miniature carver, once carved a collection of saints – in which 70 heads can be clearly seen – on a cherry stone.

In 1869, a patent was filed in London for a lavatory seat which had tiny rollers on the top to prevent anyone from standing on it.

I'll Never Forget What's-his-name

The trouble with learning things is that you forget them. Especially when it comes to using the knowledge that you need: a little gremlin pops up in the mind and eats various words, leaving you with a daft version of the truth. For instance, when you're called to stand up and recite a poem, you can end up jabbering things like: '*Tiger, tiger . . . bright, In the . . . night, What immortal . . . eye, Could . . thy fearful cemetery(?)?*' or: '*To be or not to be, that is the answer, Whether to suffer the swings and arrows of courageous torture . . .*'

Here we come to another wonderful aspect of *More Crazy-But True!* It doesn't really *matter* if you leave out bits of the curious information when you're using it – it still sounds mad or peculiar! People who stagger under the sudden mental blow of hearing a strange fact, such as 'gripe water contains more alcohol than beer or sherry' will still stagger if you get it wrong and say: '. . . water contains more alcohol than . . . sherry.' (They've probably been drinking too much sherry, anyway, which accounts for their staggering so much.)

So read on, and relax in the knowledge that you don't have to learn every bit by heart. To be on the safe side, though, it might be best to carry this book with you all the time, and read aloud from it, so as to get all the facts right. That's by far the best way of remembering things . . .

Charles Dickens, annoyed that his statue wasn't shown at Madame Tussaud's Waxworks in London, started the rumour that a fabulous reward awaits anybody who spends the night alone in the Chamber of Horrors. Though the legend still exists, no such reward was ever offered.

The most used letter in the English language is 'e'.

A man named Burhrahm, a member of the Indian Thugee Fraternity, murdered 1,150 people in 40 years.

In March 1944, faced with death in a blazing RAF bomber, Sergeant Alkemade jumped without a parachute from a height of 18,000 feet. He landed without serious injury in a ten-foot snowdrift.

The last words of Lord Palmerston were: 'Die, my dear doctor? Why, that's the last thing I shall do.'

The Vinegar River (El Rio Vinagre) in Colombia contains eleven parts of sulphuric acid and nine parts of hydrochloric acid in every thousand, and is so bitter that no fish can live in it.

A Prairie Dog isn't a dog – it's a large rodent.

The needle of the compass does not point to the North Pole. It points to the Magnetic Pole, which is 1,500 miles west of the true North Pole.

Lord Nelson, Britain's greatest admiral, suffered from acute sea-sickness throughout his life.

The most dangerous insect in the world is the common house fly. It can pass on to man more than sixty diseases and parasites.

The Niagara Falls only fall during the day. At night, the waters are diverted to power a hydro-electric plant.

Among the curious names listed in the New York telephone directory are: Mona Lisa Gooseberry, Oscar Asparagus, Peculiar Smith, Sistine Madonna McClung, Virgin Mary Smith, and Lizzie Izabitchie.

King Gustav III of Sweden believed coffee to be highly poisonous. So a convicted murderer at the King's court was ordered to drink himself to death on coffee. He lived to be 83.

Six large fire-flies would provide enough light to read this book by.

An elephant's trunk can carry 2 gallons of water.

In 1974, a thousand pigs went berserk near Devizes, in Wiltshire. They ate the fabric of a light aeroplane, seven wooden gates, $2\frac{1}{2}$ tons of hay, a straw rick, 10 cwt of cattle cake, 500 yards of electric wire, and 17 acres of cabbages.

The dead outnumber the living on earth by approximately 30 to 1.

In Hollywood, some sets used as backgrounds in Western films are made to three-quarters scale, so as to make the heroes seem larger than life.

A pound of feathers weighs more than a pound of gold. This is because feathers are weighed by 'avoirdupois' weight, which has 16 ounces to the pound, whereas gold is always weighed by 'troy' weight, which only contains 12 ounces to the pound.

In 1908, the Leaning Tower of Pisa officially weighed 14,486 tons. Sixty-six years later, in 1974, it weighed only 14,202 tons.

Henry Lewis, a Liverpool billard player, used to play with his nose instead of a cue. In 1928, he made a break of 46 points in this way.

The most costly dress ever made was worn by Marie de Medici, Queen of France, in 1622. The dress was embroidered with 3,000 diamonds and 39,000 pearls – at today's values it would be worth £6,000,000. The Queen only wore the dress once, then discarded it.

A 55-year-old Polish man, Jan Dbworski, died in Stoke-on-Trent in 1966 from choking on a garlic clove he had left in his mouth overnight to ward off Dracula-type monsters.

Only six people were killed in the Great Fire of London in 1666.

The Archer fish of India catches insects by squirting water at them from its mouth and drowning them. It has a range of about 5 feet.

The female starfish produces 2 million eggs a year. 99 per cent of them are eaten by other fish.

American scientists have invented a compound called 'Cyclophosphamide', which, when fed to sheep over a period of a few months, allows the whole fleece to be taken off like a pullover.

One morning in 1798, as Czar Paul I of Russia was inspecting his guards, he was infuriated by a soldier's cloak button, which hadn't been polished. In a rage the Czar ordered: 'About turn – march!' When asked where to, he shouted: 'To Siberia!' The 400 men dutifully set off on the 2,000 mile march – and were never heard of again.

The Indian ruler Khanjahan enjoyed handshaking with his subjects so much that when he died he left orders to be buried in a conical tomb – with his hand stuck out through the wall. Every visitor to the tomb shook hands with the corpse. Eventually, 35 years later, the hand withered away.

Atilla the Hun, leader of the hordes of Barbarians who overran much of Europe, was a dwarf, just 3 feet 4 inches tall.

The religion of the Todas people of India sternly forbids them to cross any kind of bridge. Therefore they must always swim across rivers.

When the city of St Pierre in Martinique was destroyed by an earthquake in 1908, only Augustia Ciparis, in jail for a minor offence, survived – out of a population of over 30,000 people.

One ounce of oil can cover an area of 8 acres with a fine film.

The first Duke of Marlborough was allergic to cabbage.

The owl is the only creature able to turn its head in a complete circle.

There are no such things as double-joints. Limbs that possess very flexible qualities are merely the result of stretched ligaments.

Pepsi-Cola was originally invented, by Dr Pemberton in 1886, as a cure for hangovers.

The common cold is estimated to cost the world's economy more than £10,000,000,000 a year in lost work time.

The initial wind velocity of a human sneeze is more than Gale Force 10.

Twist Your Tongue Around These

William Shakespeare, the Bard of Avon, once said 'What's in a name?' Which was pretty silly of him, for everybody knows that all there is in a name are letters of the alphabet. (But then, Will wasn't all that good at names – he couldn't even spell his own correctly! In his manuscripts he spelt it both 'William Shakespere' and 'William Shackspeare', and in his will, he spelt it 'Wm Shakespeyere'. More on this subject later – and that's a threat.)

Names and words have always intrigued people – that is, those who could speak or write. The English language is inclined to be somewhat stingy with its letters, though a lot of European countries seem to get quite drunk on words as they squander great chunks of the alphabet. For

example, whereas the English say 'tank', the German word for it is 'schutzengrabenvernitchtungsautomobile'.

It all adds up to a feast of crazy information to baffle others with. So be prepared even to meet more difficult tongue-twisters, and peculiar quirks of the language as you delve into the following chapter . . .

The Sultan of Djocjockarte is called:
Sultan Ngkoebeowonesenopaitingalgongabgurrachsaydin-pangomodev.

In Sweden, there is a city called 'A'.

The famous French writer Rabelais once wrote a book called:

'*Antipericatametaparhengedamphicribrationes*'

'1792' is not only a number but a real name. The 1792 family is living in Coulommiers, France. There are four sons – and each is named after a month: January 1792, Februrary 1792, March 1792, and April 1792. March 1792 died in September 1924.

As well as the obvious 'quick brown fox' sentence, this one contains all the letters of the alphabet: 'Pack my box with five dozen liquor jugs'.

The oldest surname in the world is 'Katz' (from the initials of the words Kohen Tsedek). Every Katz is a priest, descending in an unbroken line from Aaron, brother of Moses, 1300 B.C.

The longest name yet given to a child was bestowed on the daughter of Arthur Pepper, a Liverpool laundryman, in 1924. The child's initials used up the whole alphabet, and her christening occupied half a day. They called her: Anna Bertha Cecelia Diana Emily Fanny Gertrude Hypatia Inez Jane Kate Louise Maud Nora Ophelia Prudence Quince Rebecca Sarah Teresa Ulysis Venus Winifred Xenephon Yetty Zeno Pepper. She was usually called Alpha Pepper for short.

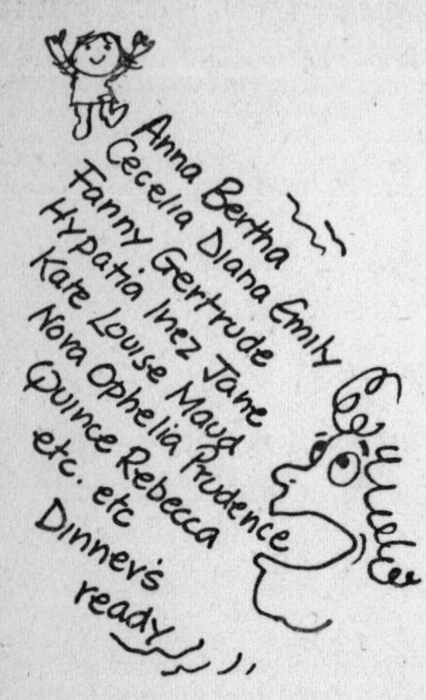

See if you can punctuate this strange-looking sentence:
'That that is is that that is not is not but that that is not is not that that is nor is that that is that that is not.'

(Here's how it's done: 'That, that is, is; that, that is not, is not; but that, that is not, is not that that is; nor is that, that is, that that is not.')
Enough of all that!

There are more than 4,000 different ways of spelling Shakespeare! And most of the literary critics who believe that Bacon wrote the plays of Shakespeare inevitably declare that the Bard was so ignorant that he could not even write his own name properly. As was pointed out in the preface to this chapter, Shakespeare spelt his name in various ways; eleven in all. Evidently there is no authentic way of spelling Will's name – here is a selection of alternatives:

Shakespeare	Shaxpur	Shakespeyere
Shakspayr	Shaxspeare	Shaxpere
Schakespear	Shakespiere	Schakespier
Shackspur	Shaxspure	Shaksper
Shakespiere	Shaxpeyere	Shaxxpeire
Shakxspur	Shakespere	Shakispeare
Schaxpeire	Shagspier	Shaxpiere etc.

The longest word that Shakespeare used, incidentally, occurs in *Love's Labour's Lost*', Act V, Scene 1, Line 44. It is: 'honorificicabilitudinity'.

The German word meaning chemist is 'gesundheitswei-derherstellungsmittelzusammenmischungsvergaltnisskud-iger'.

There is a river called 'Oo' in Africa.

The longest 12-word telegram ever sent was from Sydney Glassman, in London, in 1904. Here's how the telegram was worded:

'*Administrator-General's counter-revolutionary intercommunications uncircumstantiated Stop Quartermaster-General's disproportionableness characteristically contra-distinguished unconstitutionalist's incomprehensibilities Stop.*'

The telegram won a prize of a guinea.

In the village of Ws, in France, there is a man called Monsieur Wzs.

An advertisement for cough syrup in a French newspaper read:
'PARAMINOBENZOYLDIAETHYLAMINOAETHANALOMPHYDRO-CHLORICUM ought to be in everybody's medicine cabinet!'

The word 'nylon' is made up of abbreviated forms of New York and London; for the synthetic fibre was invented in both cities at the same time.

One of the most mis-spelt words in the English language is 'awkward'.

In Connecticut, U.S.A., there is Lake Chagoggagoggmanchuagogchaubunågungaamaug'. In the Red Indian language this means: 'You fish on your side; I fish on my side – nobody shall fish in the middle.'

In practically every language in the world, the word for 'God' has four letters. Here is a selection:

English:	LORD
Latin:	DEUS
French:	DIEU
Assyrian:	ADAT
Dutch:	GODT
German:	GOTT
Danish:	GODH
Swedish:	GOTH
Persian:	SORU
Hindu:	RAMA
Spanish:	DIOS
Greek:	TEOS
Arabic:	AMIR
Egyptian:	AMON
Inca:	PAPA
Persian:	ISTR
Portuguese:	DEUS
Japanese:	KAMI
Hindustani:	HAKK

In the Zuider Zee, Holland, there is a large bay called 'Y'.

A holy man in Benares, India, has 109 different names. The shortest of these contains 58 letters. He writes this particular name thus: Sri 88 Matparamahansaparivrajacharyaswamibikaranaandasaraswati. (We won't go into what the other 108 names are right now . . .)

In Pas de Calais, France, there is a river named 'Aa'.

Here is the world's longest swear word (you'll have to work out the meaning for yourself) – it is, of course, in German:
'Himmelherrgottkreuzmillionendonnerwetter!'

A complete copy of '*The Rubaiyat of Omar Khayyam*', measuring just $\frac{5}{16}$ of an inch square was made by James Featherstone of Yorkshire.

The late Western Empress Dowager, of China, was named: Tzuh-hsi-tuan-yu-chuang-chen-shou-klung-chin-hsein-chung-hsi-huang-tai-hou.

At the other end of the scale, a Chinaman claims to have the shortest name in the world. He is Mr I, of Hang-chow.

I Dare You To!

Few people can resist a challenge, even if they're craven cowards at heart. If you are a craven coward, welcome to the Craven Cowards Club. To brighten up a dull day, I bet you've often said to a friend something like: 'I dare you to hop along the top of that wall over there', or 'I dare you to put tomato ketchup on the art teacher's chair!' – or, 'I dare you to read *More Crazy-But True!*

If you're fond of scattering such dares around – and why not, it's fun to see somebody else making a fool of themselves – you can use the outlandish facts in this book as part of your challenge. Here are a few suggestions that could lead to riotous situations – while you watch from a safe distance. Just stroll up to a friend (or, better still, somebody you don't like), and casually say, 'I dare you to go over to that man on a donkey, and tell him statistics prove that more people die being kicked to death by donkeys than in aeroplane crashes.'

Or: 'I dare you to tell that shark that a fully-grown walrus attains a length of 12 feet, and weighs 3,000 pounds.'

Got the idea? Good – (I was getting a bit fed up with the idea myself, anyway). It's your turn now to scan the facts ahead for suitable 'dare' material.

Earthworms seven feet long are to be found in some parts of Western Australia.

The average iceberg weighs 20,000,000 tons.

Napoleon, Emperor of France and would-be ruler of the world, was terrified of cats, and would not enter a room that had one in it.

In the centre of the village of Vertud, between San Salvador and Guatemala, there is a fountain named 'Mina de Sangre' which ejects a bright red liquid that congeals like blood.

Joseph Conrad, famous author of sea-faring novels in English, was a Pole by birth, and didn't learn to speak and write a word of English till he was 47.

During 1973, over a thousand deaf viewers complained to the BBC about the bad language used by footballers on 'Match of The Day'. They were all expert lip-readers.

Thomas Parr, born in Shropshire in 1483, lived during the reigns of ten English sovereigns, dying in 1635 at the age of 132.

The epitaph of Marshal 'Shoot' Rodgers, buried at Boot Hill, Texas, reads 'Excuse My Dust'.

The Amazonian tree-frog makes its nest in the hollow of a tree from beeswax. When the bowl is full of rain-water, the frog lays its eggs, which turn into tadpoles and live in this water till they hatch into frogs.

Calves' skin makes the best vellum for lettering upon, for if a mistake is made on it, a thin layer of skin can be peeled off, leaving the writer a new surface on which to begin again.

Surfing clubs in Brisbane, Australia, recovered 250 sets of false teeth in 1974, lost by bathers and surfers in Queensland's Gold Coast holiday area.

Cyrus, King of Persia, knew the name of every soldier in his 4,000-strong army by heart.

In 1821, Maria Feodorewna, wife of Alexander III of Russia, accidentally caught sight of the following note pinned to the bottom of a death-warrant. It was in the handwriting of her husband, and read: 'Pardon impossible, to be sent to Siberia.' Maria kindly transposed the comma so that it read: 'Pardon, impossible to be sent to Siberia.' Whereupon the lucky convict was released, a free man.

Porson, a famous Greek scholar of the 18th century, could recite by heart the complete works of John Milton (author of '*Paradise Lost*') – both forward and backward.

The letter 'Q' is the French word for 'queue' – which means 'tail'. In other words, a 'Q' is an O with a tail.

Princess Anthony Kohary, of Hungary, the last of her line in 1889, was officially appointed a man.

Baptising an infant in 1971, the Rev Spinney, of Meltham, in the West Riding of Yorkshire, dipped his fingers into the holy water and scooped out six pork chops.

George Washington, first President of the United States of America, died in the last hour of the last day in the week in the last month of the last year of the 18th century.

There is no camphor in the camphor balls used to keep moths away from clothing. The balls contain naphthalene.

Ambergris – which is used as the base for the majority of the world's most expensive perfumes – comes from the intestines of diseased whales.

The first parking meters were installed in Oklahoma City in 1935.

The first aeroplane disaster was in 1920, when a plane travelling to Paris crashed in Golder's Green, London, and four people were killed.

Thomas Jefferson's famous American Declaration of Independence wasn't made on July 4th, as is commonly supposed. It was really made on July 2nd, 1776.

The Canje Pheasant, a a native of Guyana, is a kind of flying skunk: it gives off an overwhelmingly unpleasant odour in flight when frightened.

The world's rarest plant is the Small Silversword, which grows only in the crater of an extinct volcano on a Hawaiian island.

Porridge was originally a thick vegetable soup, based on leeks, nettles, and lentils.

Apes, guinea-pigs and human beings are the only mammals which are able to produce Vitamin C in their own bodies.

A herd of springboks containing an estimated 100 million animals was seen in South Africa in 1896.

The world's fastest-growing plant is Giant Kelp, a kind of seaweed. It puts on 2 feet of foliage a day.

A nephew is really a grandson! The word comes from the Latin *nepos*, and both in early English and in Latin, *nepos* means a grandchild.

The fire-brat (Latin name *Thermobius Fernorum*) is a very small flea which only lives and breeds in bakeries.

Denis Taverstock, of Lancashire, compiled a complete pack of playing cards by picking them up in the street. After collecting for 10 years, he was only 15 cards short. But it took him another 21 years to finally complete the pack in 1890.

An eye that misbehaved caused its owner, Leonard Worth, of Bristol, to shut it for one hundred days. Mr Worth spied on his neighbours in the summer of 1935, thinking they were up to no good. Stricken by conscience, he confessed his sin and begged forgiveness. The matter was talked over with a priest, and the strange penance was imposed – and Leonard duly kept one eye shut for the required one hundred days.

Each of the six husbands of Fram Irmgard Bruns, who lived in Berlin in the 1800's, committed suicide.

A telegram was sent around the world in 8 minutes in 1927.

The smallest church in the world, in Lanolia, Kentucky, seats only three people.

The river Tadjoura, on the north coast of Africa, runs backwards. It flows from the Bay of Tadjourna inland, and empties into the Lake of Assal.

There is a special newspaper for beggars published in Paris, called '*Gazette de Mendiants*'.

Countess Elizabeth Batharoy, the infamous Hungarian 'tigress', who lived from 1560-1614, killed 650 servant girls in 8 years. Being a noblewoman, she was immune from punishment.

How to Grow Hair on Bald Elbows

How, indeed – for a bald elbow is a terrible handicap to live with. But don't panic – the solution is as easy as falling off a volcano. Simply sprinkle hair-restorer on the elbow, whilst chanting a crazy, but factual, piece of information. Such as: 'Mialai Ishael, emperor of Morocco in the 18th century, had 886 children – 548 boys and 338 girls.'

Here are some other miracles you can perform with this book of crazy information close at hand:

How To Make Your Own Frankenstein Monster: Construct a horrible body of fibreglass and doughnuts, and chant fifty fabulous facts backwards to the beast. The monster will walk, talk, and tango.

How To Lose Weight: Eat two pieces of crazy information for dinner, and a page-number for pudding.

How To Score Goals At Football: Quote a staggering

piece of information to the goalkeeper just before you kick the ball at him.

How To Discover A New Continent: Leave the planet.

How To Regain Your Sanity After Reading This Book: Impossible! But a course of underwater hypnotism might well do the trick.

At a certain point in the San Juan river, U.S.A., it is possible to fish in four states: Utah, Colorado, Arizona, and New Mexico.

In the 17th century, a kind of football was played by the Matani savages of West Africa – using a human skull for a ball.

A melon weighing 50 pounds and measuring 4 feet in circumference, was grown by Mr D. Harper of Derbyshire in 1955.

Sultan Murad IV inherited 240 wives when he assumed the throne of Turkey in 1744. He decided to dispense with their services by the simple method of putting each wife in a sack and tossing them one by one into the Bosphorus.

A snake at London Zoo was fitted with a glass eye.

Early Victorian tram-hauling steam engines were disguised as horses, so as not to frighten the real horses in the streets.

This is the riddle that caused the death of Homer in his vain attempt to solve it – as recorded in the classic '*Plutarch's Lives*':

What we caught,
We threw away,
What we couldn't catch,
We kept.

The answer to the riddle – a flea.

One out of every four species of mammal is a bat.

An out-of-work Anglican minister went to his local employment exchange in Hull, Yorkshire, and was offered the post of Moslem religious leader in Cardiff, South Wales.

Richard the Lionheart spent only four months of his life in England.

A salesman who admitted a speeding offence wrote to Wigan magistrates, explaining that his speedometer had been steamed up by the hot black puddings he was carrying at the time. He was fined £10.

When a submarine was invented by Dutchman Cornelius van Drebel, in 1624, the British Admiralty scoffed at the invention, and are on record as saying that it was 'a damn silly, trifling novelty that will never catch on'.

The air above one acre of ground weighs approximately 40,000,000 tons.

Tamerlane, a Turkish chieftain of the 14th century, ordered 120 large pyramids to be built after a successful battle. Each pyramid contained 80,000 heads of the defeated army.

The monarch of Britain hasn't always been addressed as 'Your Majesty'. First it was 'Your Grace', then 'Your Excellent Grace', then 'High and Mighty Prince'. The first English king to be called 'Your Majesty' was Henry VIII.

In a recent popularity poll conducted by Madame Tussauds's Waxworks in London, Dr Crippen tied with Enoch Powell for fifth place in the 'Hate and Fear' section.

Mules were once used to haul trams up the hills of Denver, Colorado, U.S.A. As an incentive, they were allowed to ride on the platform for the downward run. A farmer who bought one of these mules for ploughing, found that, whenever he reached the crest of a hilly field, the mule would immediately try to jump aboard the plough.

It has been scientifically proved that fog doesn't deaden the sound of traffic, or indeed any sound at all.

In China, as well as rickshaws, enormous versions of wheelbarrows are used to transport people. Pulled by one man, they hold up to a dozen passengers.

The first woman elected to the House of Commons was Constance, Countess of Markiewicz. She became the member for St Patrick's, Dublin, in 1918, but for some mysterious reason, never took her seat.

After a long bout of drinking vodka in May 1947, Ivan Stobb, a Russian workman, tried to blow out a match with which he'd just lit a cigarette. Flames shot from his mouth, and bystanders heard a muffled explosion from within him. Then Ivan Stobb dropped down dead.

Scuba-diving gets its name from the initials of the equipment used for the sport, which was called Self-Contained Underwater Breathing Apparatus.

The patron saint of thieves is St Nicholas.

The valuable fur known as nutria comes from the Giant Coypu rat.

More people live in Asia than in all the other continents put together.

Whalebone isn't a bone at all. It is baleen, and is a substance attached to a whale's upper jaws.

Treasure said to be worth £300,000,000 is said to lie at the bottom of Lake Cordillera, in the Guatavita Mountains, Colombia, South America.

750 million Christmas cards are posted in the United Kingdom yearly.

One inch of rainfall weighs 100 tons an acre.

There are over 40,000 direct descendants of Confucius (551-478 B.C.) living in China.

Professor Rask, of Copenhagen University, could speak 235 languages fluently. He also compiled and published 28 different language dictionaries.

Ten per cent of the earth's land surface is covered with debris left by Ice Age glaciers.

Bhutan, a tiny country that lies in the Himalayas, has issued postage stamps that sing and talk. The ultra-miniature records within the stamps sing the Bhutanese national anthem, folk songs, and give the history of the country.

Meteorologists, for some strange reason, have nothing to do with the study of meteorites. They are concerned with atmospheric conditions in relation to weather and climate.

One egg of the great auk – which became extinct in 1844 – was sold at auction in 1930 for £330. Today the egg would fetch about £1,500.

Three men who were hanged, for the murder of a magistrate, on Greenberry Hill, London, in 1641, were named Green, Berry, and Hill.

The 'Kyaik-Hto-Yo' pagoda in Burma is built on a huge boulder which stands on the brink of a 2,000 foot chasm. The local natives believe the boulder is balanced on a single hair from the head of Buddha.

Wormwood has nothing to do with worms or wood. The name comes from the Anglo-Saxon word 'werm-wod', meaning 'man-inspiring' and 'a good tonic'.

Henry VI succeeded to the throne of England and France in 1422 at the age of 8 months.

Think of a Number from 1 to 997,864,245,886

There's a kind of magic about numbers that makes one think of fish and chips, or the design of croquet mallets. (The very first croquet mallets, by the way, were invented in the early 15th century, and were made of solid pig-iron.) Which has nothing at all to do with numbers – but then, neither has Miss Joyce Wethered, of Sussex, who, whilst playing golf in 1959, hit a swallow with a long drive, whereupon the ball bounced off the bird on to the green, and ran into the hole. What you might call getting two birdies in one.

But to return to numbers, which must be pretty tired of waiting for us. Numbers come in all shapes and sizes, usually beginning at 0 and often going on to incredible lengths. It's said that numbers never lie, but they often make you think they do. This is because they have a rather peculiar sense of humour. In this section of the book you'll find all sorts of crazy combinations of figures, some of which will make you dizzy just looking at them. If this happens, just lie down in a shaded room with an ice-block and a copy of this book on your head.

Just in case the pages ahead should look uncomfortably like a maths lesson, you'll find some random crazy information here and there, such as the pilot-less French aeroplane, and the famous last words of Lord Byron. So go ahead – toddle in, and see if it doesn't all add up.

The common garden wood-louse (which can roll itself into a tight ball) used to be given by medieval doctors to patients suffering from gout or palsy.

170,141,183,460,469,229,731,687,303,715,884,105,727 is the largest number that cannot be divided by any other.

James Lanvier, of Edinburgh, sneezed 1,690 times in succession in 1928.

A gallon of vinegar weighs more in winter than in summer.

The most persistent number there is, mathematically, is: 526,315,789,473,684,210. You may multiply this figure with any number you choose, but the original figures will always appear in the result.

Lord Byron's famous last word was: 'Goodnight.'

Light travels from the sun at a speed of 186,325 miles per second. It takes eight and a half minutes to reach the earth.

The following mathematical puzzle is told in connection with the invention of chess. An East Indian Potentate was so pleased with the game that he promised the inventor – a slave – the fulfilment of any wish. The slave asked for the number of grains of wheat which would result if one grain was placed on the first square of the chess board, two on the second, four on the third, eight on the fourth, etc. – each time twice as many as on the last square.

At first glance, this wish seemed to be a modest one. But calculations showed that it would be impossible for the Potentate to keep his promise, even if he owned the entire earth and spent his whole life growing wheat on it. For the result is: 18 quintillions, 446 quadrillions, 744 trillions, 73 billions, 709 millions, 551,615 grains.

During a storm in Lapleau, France, in 1968, lightning struck a sheep fold, killing all the black sheep, but leaving all the white ones unharmed.

The Mountain Devil, a lizard-like creature which lives in Australia, never drinks. It absorbs tiny drops of dew through its skin.

Lord Edward Russell gave a party in London in 1807 where 6,000 men got drunk. A large fountain was used as a punch bowl, into which 800 gallons of brandy were poured. Among the other ingredients were 70 gallons of rum, 20,000 lemons, 1,400 pounds of sugar, and 50 ground nutmegs.

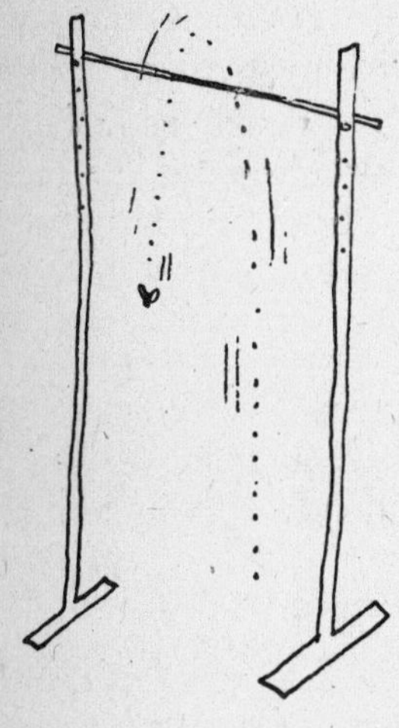

A flea can jump 200 times its own height.

A Russian woman, Eva Vassilet, gave birth in her lifetime to 16 pairs of twins, 7 sets of triplets, and 4 sets of quads – a grand total of 69 children.

There are 2,161 crown princes – all heir to the throne in succession – in Arabia.

Graham Laine of Chicago, U.S.A., has a collection of 480 antique chamber pots, valued at over £20,000.

A thunderbolt isn't a solid object which falls from the sky. It is merely the result of lightning striking something and fusing it by its intense heat.

In most Arab tribes it is considered polite – even a compliment to the chef – to belch loudly after a meal. On Arabian television in 1974, during a commercial for a soft drink, the actor drank, beamed happily – then belched.

142857 is something of a mystic number. All the figures of the sum appear when multiplied as follows:

142857 × 2 = 285714
142857 × 3 = 428571
142857 × 4 = 571428
142857 × 5 = 714285
142857 × 6 = 857142

But thereafter, a completely different result appears:

142857 × 7 = 999999

Here's a rather difficult little problem:

$$9^9$$

The above figure expresses 9 raised to the 9th power of 9, or 9 raised to the 387,420,489th power. It is the largest sum that can be indicated with two figures.

The final answer will contain 369 million digits. Allowing for 5 digits to the inch, the length of paper required to write down the answer in a single line would be 1,164 miles. It would also take about 150 years to complete the task. (The problem has yet to be fed to a computer, probably for fear of blowing a fuse!)

Oliver Cromwell was hanged four days after he died.

The last will and testament of Rabelais, the famous French writer, read simply: 'I have nothing. I owe much. The rest I leave to the poor.'

In 1907, a rainfall of 907 inches was recorded in the Khasi Hills, Africa.

Mrs Alice Cosby, a telephonist from Hull in Yorkshire, has memorised over 2,000 telephone numbers.

All the books of the Bible and the Talmud contain no more than 6,654 different words – including derivatives.

The so-called elements – fire, water, earth and air – aren't elements at all. They are compounds.

Here's a rather strange-looking piece of addition:

```
 123456789
 987654321
 123456789
 987654321
         2
──────────
2222222222
──────────
```

A French aeroplane, invented in 1934, flew without the aid of a pilot. It took off and landed completely under radio-control.

The Battle of Hastings (1066) wasn't fought at Hastings at all. It took place six miles away at Senlac Hill.

Queen Anne (1702-1774) bore a total of 17 children – and outlived every one of them.

The present Emperor of Japan, Hirohito, is the 124th emperor of the same family, maintaining an unbroken line which has lasted for 2,635 years.

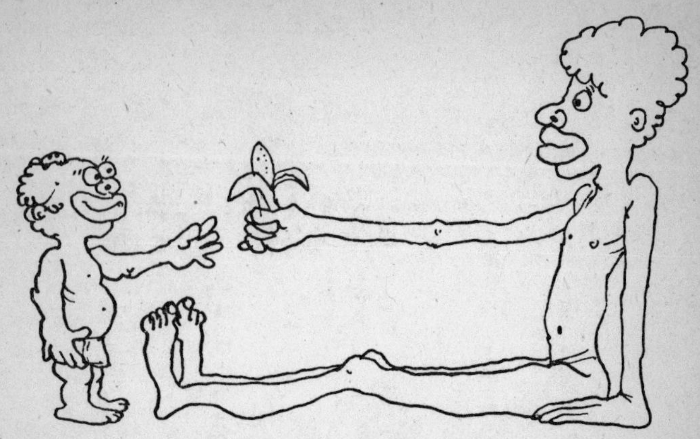

The smallest and the tallest people in the world live in Africa. The men of the Batutsi tribe average 7 feet 4 inches in height – and the men of the Pygmy tribe grow to an average of 4 feet 1 inch.

The Atlas moth of India has a wing-span of 12 inches.

Embedded in the 'Begbic' glacier in British Columbia is the perfectly preserved body of a man who was trapped in the ice over a century ago. The body has been seen countless times in the slow-moving river of ice, and experts have estimated that it will reach a point where it can be recovered for burial in 1982.

An old tribal law forbids an Australian aborigine to speak to his mother-in-law: it is believed to bring bad luck.

On the island of Novaya Sibir, in Siberia, there is a fire that was started in 1951 by a careless hunter. The fire is still burning, fed by coal close to the earth's surface.

An 8-feet tall giant, Thomas Jenkins, a clerk at the Bank of England, who died in 1798, requested that to foil body-snatchers, he be buried in the safest place he knew – on the Bank's premises. His wish was carried out, and Jenkins's corpse is still there today.

Liu Ch'ung, a Chinese government official in the 15th century, was born with a double pupil in each eye.

Square tomatoes and apples were especially grown by a Yorkshire farmer in 1974.

Let's See How Crazy You Really Are

Were you awake when you read this book? Or, at least, when you *began* reading it? For if you did happen to slumber all the way through, you're in trouble. You've reached the part where you're going to be ruthlessly quizzed on the information so thickly planted on these pages. (On the other hand, if you were asleep, then you're probably still asleep, so it doesn't matter. Sweet dreams.) If by some lucky chance you're awake, here are your instructions (read, memorise, then eat them):

The Crazy Quiz is split into two sections. In Section One, you have to select the correct answer from the four alternatives given. And in Section Two, all you do is answer True or False to the statements made. Don't read the answers first. You might get a higher score that way, but remember that honesty is the best policy and that the early bird catches the worm. But then, who wants worms?

Oh, go on, then – look at the answers first. But if you do, you're guilty of Quiz-Cheating, and if caught, you may be sentenced to a year among the Giant Flying Tree Frogs of South America.

So be good for once. Here comes the Crazy Quiz:

SECTION ONE
The Place to be is 'A' to 'D'

1. Who invented the yo-yo?

(a) Mickey Mouse
(b) Winston Churchill
(c) Jasper Q. Munchworthy
(d) The Ancient Greeks

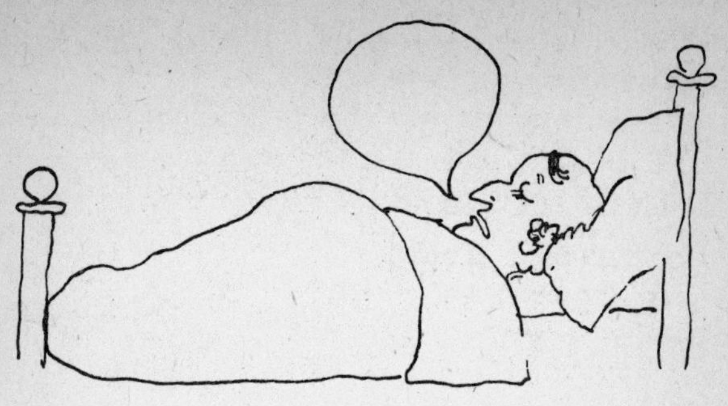

2. What were Lord Byron's last words?

(a) 'Put down that gun!'
(b) 'This porridge has a funny taste, don't you think?'
(c) 'Goodnight'
(d) 'How did Chelsea do in the Cup-Final?'

3. Where does the needle of the compass point to?

(a) Buckingham Palace
(b) The Magnetic Pole
(c) Twenty-five past eleven
(d) You

4. What did Henry Lewis, the billiard player, use for a cue?

(a) A telegraph pole
(b) The little toe on his right foot
(c) A cucumber sandwich
(d) His nose

5. What was Napoleon terrified of?

(a) Cats
(b) Prunes
(c) Josephine
(d) Knitting patterns

6. How long did Richard the Lionheart spend in England?

(a) Ten minutes
(b) Four months
(c) Seven years
(d) Seventy years

7. What do the initials S.C.U.B.A. stand for?

(a) Siberian Clumsy Underwear Boiling Association
(b) Some Cannot Understand Being Athletic
(c) Self-Contained Underwater Breathing Apparatus
(d) Sweet Custard Under Baked Apple

8. What is whalebone made out of?

(a) Dried frog's spawn
(b) Baleen
(c) Whales' bones
(d) Spitoon

9. What is the longest word that Shakespeare used?

(a) Honorificicabilitudinity
(b) Fish
(c) Blood
(d) Nunnery

10. Where did Rudyard Kipling's famous poem 'If' first appear?

(a) In the Obituary Column of *The Times*
(b) On Kipling's lavatory wall
(c) In a magazine called 'Practical Brainwashing Monthly'
(d) On the window of a garage in Mexico

SECTION TWO
True or False?

Just answer T or F to the following statements:

1. There are 12 million cells in the human brain.

2. The fastest moving snail in England is called 'Lightning'.

3. Snow isn't white.

4. The Niagara Falls only fall during the night.

5. Pepsi-Cola was invented as a cure for hangovers.

6. The word NYLON means 'New Yellow Legs Or Nothing!'

7. Apple-rind makes the best vellum for lettering on.

8. When fed a compound called 'Cyclophosphamide', sheep shed their fleeces like pullovers.

9. Earthworms seventy feet long live in Australia.

10. The speed of a sneeze is over Gale Force 10

11. The world's rarest plant is the dandelion.

12. Camphor balls contain chewing-gum.

13. Princess Anthony Kohary of Hungary was a man.

14. The King of Persia knew the names of his 4,000 soldiers by heart.

15. Shakespeare once wrote: 'What's in a gnome?'

16. An iceberg can weigh up to 20 million tons.

17. Lord Nelson suffered from colour-blindness.

18. The owl can turn its head inside-out.

19. One in every five of Britain's policemen is married to a lady pole-vaulter.

20. In the 18th century, a kipper was a salted whale.

Answers

Part One

1. *d*; 2. *c*; 3. *b*; 4. *d*; 5. *a*; 6. *b*; 7. *c*; 8. *b*; 9. *a*; 10. *a*.

Part Two

1. True; 2. True; 3. True; 4. False; 5. True; 6. False; 7. False; 8. True; 9. False; 10. True; 11. False; 12. False; 13. True; 14. True; 15. False; 16. True; 17. False; 18. False; 19. False; 20. False.

Well — Just How Crazy are You?

(An assessment of your character, based on how many answers you got correct.)

30 Correct: Amazing! You must be completely crazy! The only trouble is, your brain is now such a dustbin of weird information that it probably won't be able to absorb anything useful. Still if you're as crazy as all that, doubtless you don't really care. (But remember the dustman calls on Tuesdays.)

20-25 Correct: Highly commendable. But a score that indicates that you're very smug, conceited, and over-fond of rice pudding. But your good points – kind, excellent at daft quiz games – win you a bonus piece of Crazy Information: A cat-fish isn't a fish – it's an octopus.

15-20 Correct: Very good. You obviously possess a sound mind in a healthy body, and a sense of balance that will stand you in good stead on tightropes and see-saws.

5-15 Correct: Pathetic effort. After all, the questions were quite easy, the printing unsmudged, and you had ink in your pen. But perhaps the light was dim . . . Yes, that's your only excuse – you forgot to switch on the light.

1-5 Correct: Admit it – you're stupid, and you know it.

o Correct: Oh dear. To be tactful about it, you could have done better, couldn't you? (Well, it would have been extremely skilful of you to do worse.) Tell you what – do the quiz again, and have a good look at the answers first. Make notes. Better still, have the answers in front of you as you do the quiz. So go back to the beginning of the book and start again . . .

Parsley the Lion

MICHAEL BOND

'Dill,' Parsley read, 'is a dog. He is modest . . . kind . . . a loyal friend . . . noble . . . upright . . .'

Parsley read Dill's entry for 'Who's Who' again, because it *certainly* wasn't the same dog he knew! The Dill that Parsley knew had sold him that dud car with three wheels and only a reverse gear – the same dog who pretended he owned the only television in the Herb Garden!

No, Dill definitely wasn't 'modest, noble' and all that. In fact, Parsley thought the description suited himself much better!

Parsley Parade is also an Armada Lion.